YOKED

Sex, Gin, and the Will of God

Denise Hill

<u>Dedication</u>

To those new in Christ, those who have traveled with Christ, and those who are still trying to make it in Christ – stay encouraged.

Table of Contents

Foreword

As I read various segments of this book, *Yoked*, first it brought me to tears for it allowed me to travel with the author as she took her audience on her journey. It mesmerized me. I felt during some parts of the book I was paralyzed by the events that occurred as the author so vividly paints a picture that is reflective of so many that sit in the comfortable cushioned chairs and pews in many of our churches today.

This book is by no means fictional but rather factual. As a matter of fact the picture painted by the author will bring not only conviction as to where I am in the process but how can I do better in fulfilling the *P*urpose, *P*lan and *D*estiny God has for my life.

Yoked will challenge the way the Gospel is presented, offering it in a more relevant manner that not only appeals to the general public but will produce action on behalf of the participant. Not only will this book liberate the religious sector but also those who may not have any sort of religious conviction. As you read this book I strongly suggest that you approach with an open mind, open heart and open spirit.

This book, **Yoked,** truly can be considered a vital resource for every avid reader, skeptic or even agnostic for it will agitate in a positive manner the internal depths of one's psyche. If you are in search of a resource, tool or easy read to recommend for a friend, family or foe, **Yoked** definitely fits the profile. You will not be disappointed. This book, **Yoked,** will be a blessing to the readers, consumers and communicators through the truth's shared by the author.

Apostle Willie Tolbert
Senior Pastor
Yes Lord Ministries
East Orange, NJ

Introduction

There was a woman who in her youth was told if she accepted Jesus as her Lord and Savior all her sins would be forgiven and her soul saved from eternity in Hell. "If Jesus came today are you sure you would go home with Him," the preacher asked. "You ought to know. You ought to know that you know that you know that you're ready to see Jesus." He continued the press. "Are you sure? If not you need to come to this altar." So the young girl did what the preacher suggested. That day she learned of salvation and accepted Jesus as her Savior. Unfortunately, she knew practically nothing else concerning this Christ she met – not His words, not His ways, not His will; nothing.

With the exception of the one-line Easter Sunday recitations of her adolescence, she knew no scriptures and she had no practical skills for studying her bible. The fact that she did not know how to talk to this Jesus she accepted was most frustrating. There was no conversation. She didn't know what to say and while others boasted, "God told me…" she could not hear Him. The familiar "now I lay me down to sleep" bedtime chant and "God is grace" meal time blessing were her only forms of prayer. Spiritually she knew nothing.

With a lack of understanding of what Christ required of her or even that there were requirements outside of simply accepting Him, she tucked away her salvation and moved forward with life, often progressing into a life of sin and destructive behavior. Alcohol abuse, depression, sexual abuse, promiscuity, and excessive gambling entangled her life. By adulthood she was "used goods," both emotionally and physically damaged. Dissatisfied and longing for something more, a series of events exposed the mess in her life that had become normalcy.

Broken, vulnerable, connected to destructive acts, and toxic people, God called this young woman into a relationship that began with that faithful altar call in her youth. She journeyed years through life before realizing her lack of intimately knowing Him did not determine His love for her, or His purpose for her life and life experiences. Already helping others, Christ wanted her to meet greater needs but needed her bound to Him and not the issues and sin that was consuming her life. This is the revelation of "Yoked."

A true and life-changing encounter is what I experienced at age 13 when I accepted Christ, only to feel spiritually abandoned and emotionally empty. No one took me aside and mentored me into an understanding of salvation or counseled me on how to have a relationship with Him. There were only hypocritical judgments and condemning looks when fallen short of the image of a "good girl." With a lack of knowledge I knew only to act out the "church folk" examples set before me while secretly clinging to the need to once again experience that indescribable feeling of freedom experienced at salvation. The chase for an encore performance was fruitless in the church but glimpses of that freedom were felt through gin, men, and race tracks. The weight of maintaining <u>my</u> way of life became burdensome and undesirable. The feeling I longed for similar to the excitement and joy felt at 13 fleeted and was no longer found in anywhere. In its place was excruciating pain from the inside out tearing between where I was and where I should be.

I needed to return to the Christ I committed to in my youth. I needed to return not to church, but to the same Christ who was so loudly calling me out of my stuff and so I did. I entered into a renewed covenant with God. However, that return was not enough to appease His correcting and disciplining, one of the most difficult and painful places to be in Christ. Divinely separated from familiar friends, comfortable things, and popular places, God's chastening sought to clean out everything in my past and present that yoked me to darkness and not to His will for my life.

After the euphoria of salvation fades and the frantic pace to learn everything church slows, many of us spend a season separate from the will and commandments of Christ becoming yoked to sin, the desire of selves, the world, and Satan. The degree of rebellion varies per individual ranging from something as simple as no longer attending church and fellowshipping as Christ commands, to the more severe drug addictions and sexual perversions. Some still reluctantly dwell in this state finding it difficult to acknowledge a yoke, not to mention breaking it and picking up a true relationship with Him. Yet all who truly had an encounter with the living God eventually reach a point where the desire to drink, drug, club, or jump from bed to bed become physically ineffective as well as emotionally and psychologically unfulfilling. The exhaustion of both running from God and bearing the heavy yoke of the world become too great. With no one and nothing else to seek we reach a crossroads where we surrender and seek God or die.

Since birth and our demanding cries for bottles and attention, to our present adult state of always getting our way, our selfish wants have often outweighed the terms of our covenant with Christ. The agreement made at the time we accepted Jesus as our Lord and Savior becomes breached. Fortunately, his mercy covers us but in that state just enough weight of our unrighteousness is returned to our shoulders to carry. What we like to do and what we choose to indulge in (our flesh) have held and continues to hold many hostage – bound by and yoked to sin.

Often we hear the word sin and are programmed to only consider the most egregious of acts, such as fornication, murder, homosexuality, or drug and alcohol abuse. We dare not consider that our gossiping, over shopping, sharp tongue, or laziness as sin. In the eyes of Christ our "smallest" sin is equal to what we define as a "big" one. Therefore "Yoked" is as relevant to the evangelist who loves and lives for Christ, but is impatient with her children as it is to the person who prostitutes themselves for crack. We all must consider if what we are yoked to may be hindering our growth in the kingdom of God and in life.

As I grew, Christ began to show me how it is not about our individuality and what <u>we</u> want, desire, or feel. We are not islands. You are now kingdom beings and part of one body. Our thoughts are not our own, and our actions should not be decided by our emotions or physical desires. Accepting Christ means accepting His likes, His dislikes, and His desires and accepting them as our own. We become yoked or bound to His will for our life, His commandments, His love, and the benefits of being His sons and are expected to walk together with Him in that understanding. Our emotions and personal requirements often tell us the burden of such a yoke is huge and that maintaining a life of relationship and right standing (righteousness) is difficult to say the least. But the burden of Christ is light compared to the cost of sin, and our longing to please the Father makes our responsibilities to His word bearable.

"Yoked" is a word concerning the lifestyles of the saints, those who, at a time in their life had a divine encounter where they sincerely accepted Christ as their Lord and Savior, even if not currently in line with God's word. It is for those who are saved and out of His will, for those who have been out for a while and feel a pull back to Christ not "church", and also for those who recall being out there and have returned to Christ but seek perspective on their experience. It speaks to how we view our salvation and the state of rebellion that results from our lack of relationship and broken covenant with the Father. "Yoked" is about the process God uses to return us from our state of rebellion and sin back to His will for our life.

Daily we must remain conscious of our covenant with Christ that we might successfully fulfill it. If our actions, thoughts, and desires are not in line with Christ they are in line with Satan. Even in a state of doing what pleases our self (flesh) and not perceiving to be overtly in line with Satan, is contrary to being yoked with Christ. If we are not yoked to His will we are, by default yoked to sin. There is no middle ground and no gray area. It is hot or cold. Not lukewarm (Rev. 3:16).

Please note – this book is not an indictment against the church or the clergy. This is not an accusation of any failings of the church. It is not a biography for the purposes of telling my business. "Yoked" is not my way of playing Pastor. I am in no way offering counsel concerning any individual situation but rather perspective and an understanding based on my personal experiences that I pray will bless those who can relate.

I do not perceive to have arrived. I am still a student of the living Word. I understand as long as I am flesh I will continue to battle with flesh and have the need to evaluate and re-evaluate my standing in Him. Still I offer you the example of my personal experiences to draw from during your spiritual walks with and without Christ. I encourage you to use them to consider and examine your lifestyle confirming your walk is reflective of whom you are yoked.

Chapter One

THERE MUST BE MORE TO THIS

I got saved at the age of 13 not in an intimate meeting with a Pastor who could explain spiritual commitment to me. I did not accept Christ in my living room pressing my hand against the television during a call to salvation on Christian television, where I could continue watching for guidance and understanding. Rather I got saved in one of those mass savings where "the doors of the church are open" for everyone attending to enter in. There were always plenty such opportunities available to me. I sang with the region's largest and most popular community choir, affectionately called Youth for Christ. There was an endless array of concerts to perform in, countless churches to visit, and each opportunity ensured the predictable altar call. Altar calls often seemed like another part of the ritual of church rather than an honest attempt to win souls but one evening I chose to take part. After all, in the middle of all my religious activities, I still had not accepted Jesus as my

Savior and confessed my sins so by definition I was not saved. I simply went to church and sang gospel music.

"Every head bowed and every eye closed," was the familiar statement that began each soul pleading process. The Minister embarked on his solicitation of people who did not know Jesus as their personal Savior requesting they raise their hand then put it back down. "I see that hand, I see that hand, yes, in the back I see that hand," the Minister proclaimed. Everyone's bowed head and closed eye was supposed to hamper any embarrassment of exposing yourself as a sinner. I took solace and slipped my hand in the air then quietly lowered it into my lap. Before I could clasp my hands I heard, "I see that hand."

I wanted to know this Christ I had been singing about for so long and felt secure in my passive admission of needing Him. Having witnessed countless altar calls before one would think the next step would not surprise me but it did. Of all those who raised their hands a second more public act was requested; "stand up and walk to the altar for prayer." The reason for the congregation bowing their heads and closing their eyes became completely mute as everyone raised their heads to see who was moving towards the altar. Their golf clap in celebration did nothing to comfort my feeling of betrayal. Obligated to the process

I began, I rose to my feet and took the longest walk a person could experience. It felt as though each step drew more eyes to my exposed and naked soul. Somehow I made it. There standing with several others to repeat, verbatim, a prayer of confession.

"Lord I love you…I accept you as my Lord and Savior…I believe that you died on the cross and rose on the third day…Lord, I am a sinner…I ask that you come into my heart and forgive my sins…"

At the conclusion I was saved, I think. At least, that was what we at the altar were told. That was the only thing I was told.

I could now profess that Jesus was my personal Lord and Savior. I had entered into an eternal covenant or agreement with Him that I was His and His commandments would guide my life. I had become yoked to Christ.

Yoked

A yoke in the natural is a harness that binds and constrains two animals, usually oxon, together by the neck. If a stronger animal is attached to a weaker one the weaker, because bound, is submissive to the will of the stronger.

Whether we are aware or not, as members of the body of Christ we have professed to be bound to the will of our Savior, Jesus Christ. As such our obligation to the vow we took during our time of salvation is to obey His commandments and fulfill His purpose for us in the Earth. However, our churches and communities are filled to capacity with members who have accepted Jesus and who are essentially good people who try to live right according to the commandments of God they are familiar with. Do not kill. Do not commit adultery. And love your parents. Unfortunately, they live in a state of spiritual ignorance content with learning solely what is taught over the pulpit or spoken in the microphone. Such was my case after salvation.

Though saved and connected with Christ as my Savior, I still knew nothing of Him. Not His likes or dislikes, not His purpose for my life, and not any of His words other than the scripture clichés like "cleanliness is next to godliness" or "if you take one step He'll take two." Neither of which is in the bible. I remember thinking, 'there must be more to this saved thing.' Out of everything the piece most noticeably missing in the puzzle called my life was Him. I never felt His touch. I never personally felt His presence. Obviously everyone but me felt "the Spirit."

Family, choir members, even visitors danced with joy, ran in excitement, and shouted praises uncontrollably. They had a hold of the elusive "holy ghost." Yes, everyone seemed to feel Him but me.

Finally my time to physically feel this Jesus I met and sang about would come. I remember it so clearly, it was at a concert featuring the late Rev. James Moore about a year or two after my moment at the altar. After he concluded singing he ministered a bit before conducted an altar call different from any I had witnessed before. He invited folks to come to the altar and with just a shake of his hand, feel the awesome power he was under. He called it "the anointing." The memory of my last long walk to the altar initially caused fear and doubt to press my feet to the floor but a strange blend of curiosity and desire loosened their hold. Wanting to grasp this life changing promise I took the Reverend up on his offer. First there were baby steps toward the front of the church, before waiting patiently behind a crowd of people, then some people, then a few of people, then there I was, with no specific expectations but a longing to have something happen.

I stretched out my hand. The Minister, with a microphone in one hand and sweat rolling from his forehead pass an intense almost trace like expression round the curve of his chin, quickly grabbed my young hand with his free hand…then released.

The next few seconds seemed like an eternity as my mind processed the brief encounter. He shook my hand so quickly. Did he do anything? Did he hurry me alone because I was young? With all the shouting and dancing and crying around me it seems like everyone else had a response. Where was mine? What was I supposed to feel? Why was there nothing? Then suddenly, returning to the pew, something electric and barely describable overtook me. It was as if a separate person inside of me was jolted with electricity. Running through her body was the energy of overwhelming joy so much so this inside person needed to jump and ran and dance to express it. My physical body quickly followed suit of my emotions and began to jump and run and dance up the aisle. While I wanted to worry about what others thought that same person inside did not care. She shouted through the church until the body holding her, my body, got tired. The exhaustion left me slumped over and crying.

I felt it. I felt Him. I felt free. Not sure how or what happened outside of the religious explanation of finally "catching the Holy Spirit." And though I felt like this other person in me had the experience and I was simply along for the ride, I made the encounter my own. It was my first personal encounter with Jesus and it was unforgettable. "Wow" could not describe it. I wanted more. I had to feel that electricity again. I desired to taste that consuming joy again.

Unfortunately no one took the time to teach me how to hold on to that feeling. There was no one who pulled me aside afterward and explained the details of it all. There were hundreds of witnesses to my breakthrough – choir members, family, friends, even my mother – all I perceived were experienced at feeling His presence yet no one sought to shield me from spiritual ignorance. They discussed even joked about the intricacies of my praise and who I looked like when I danced but nothing more. Did they believe that having witnessed countless others shout and dance I was fully aware of what occurred in my life? Did they think my early teen maturity was sufficient in comprehending the encounter? Did they assume I would be able to repeat the experience on my own?

I was not certain what they believed or if there was any thought or awareness at all to my plight. They did not offer and in their defense I did not ask. I began to think it better to have never felt Him then to have met Him, felt Him, yet still live without Him. As time passed my physical body matured but my spiritual body and that inner dancing lady remained a babe. Ironically I continued to sing with choirs and community groups constantly remaining in a religious atmosphere. Several times a week I was in a church. That was the one place Jesus was supposed to be and the one place others around me appeared to continue feeling His spirit. So I stayed there, singing inspiration to others before myself leaving uninspired and unmoved. Time passed. I grew in His word but not in relationship. More time passed and there would be no other visits from Him to me. The memory of my one encounter would have to sustain for years.

Accepting Christ and feeling His presence still availed no emphasis on personal relationship or education of His word. There is a proverb Solomon gives that many overlook as a scriptural cliché but offers great guidance. Proverbs 3:5-6 reads:

(5) Trust in the Lord with all your heart,
And lean not on your own understanding;
(6) In all your ways acknowledge Him,
And He shall direct your path.

This scripture speaks not only to our faith and belief that God has the situations we cannot comprehend under His perfect control, but it is direction to establish a relationship with God that will dictate our thoughts, perspectives, and actions throughout life. We cannot just live off the understanding we have nor that of our Pastors and Ministers. More importantly we cannot survive or prosper under our own understanding of what the life or the ways of a Christ representative should be. As long as we are in our fleshly states, our understanding and our thoughts are tainted. My testimony gives example to the fact that salvation does not bring instant knowledge and you cannot just shout it out. Establishing the connection between we the sons and He the Father does not make us immediately like Him. Rather salvation is meant to begin a relationship. To begin a process of growing and maturing with He in us and we in Him, through study and communication, until we are completely reflective of Christ.

No Relationship

After meeting Christ and having no relationship with Him, I also met a guy and began the relationship of a lifetime. Sophomore year of high school kicked into full swing and I was more than ready to become a full fledged social butterfly. Teen society dictated it was time to go out, have a real date, and pursue my first true love. That is where "Damon" came in. He was not too tall, like the basketball players I was used to, and not too short, like the men my sister took to. He was just right with cute eyes and a nice, lean, but well defined body. Already familiar and smitten with him from middle school, I was pleased with our advancing relationship.

Homecoming preparations were made early in the school year by others. I saw no personal purpose in planning. Having missed the previous year's dance, I was sure to sit at home once again. That was not my desire, however. After all, there was finally a brother I was getting emotionally closer to day by day. I would love the opportunity to dress up like a tomboy princess and go to the ball with my prince and help to achieve my goal was but a bedroom away; my older sister. She and I had a good chance at gaining our very protective father's permission to participate in Homecoming night festivities if we banded together.

Our plan worked and the evening was wonderful. "Damon" and I spent the night holding hands and gazing into each other's eyes. He could not take his eyes off me. That was the first time he, and many of my friends ever saw me in something other than my jeans or basketball and track sweats. My hair was hooked up and my face made up. I was looking good by anyone's standards but "Damon" was the only opinion I cared about.

Every glance, every smile, every caress of my hand drew my young heart deeper into a world of intense emotions. Was it love? I had no clue but was completely open and at peace with exploring the territory.

My sister and her boyfriend, now seniors, wanted to leave the parentally authorized dance to get some one on one time. You would find no objection from us. There was a mutual longing to be alone with each other and our emotions. Leaving the dance early we hopped in the car, and drove to a popular date spot; the airport.

National Airport in Washington, DC had a nice lot right by the waters of the Potomac River where you could load your boat into the water, go fishing, or just park and watch the planes take off and land right over your head. In our little world the roaring of jet engines flying through the night sky over the placid water was as tranquil as climbing to the top of a mountain and looking out over a blossomed meadow at the looming sunset as it changes the sky every colorful shade in the rainbow during a clear summer evening. It was beautiful. We sat on the hood of the car holding hands and talking for hours. This was not just childish gibberish. We talked to each other about things we never shared with anyone else in a way that was completely unique to us. It was effortless. Finally there was someone who cared about my feelings and thoughts. Family, sports, friends, favorite things, dreams, career goals...no subject was off limits. Before we knew it we were talking about our feelings for each; feelings which had strengthened through the night.

Our emotions were at an all time high but still completely indescribable. There was a moment of silence... a moment where we just lay on the hood of the car looking at the stars, marinating in our own personal peace while sharing each other's presence. We seemed to breathe together, inhaling and exhaling at the same pace, our heart beating to the same tempo. With all the words we previously shared suddenly we needed no words to know each other's thoughts. We also knew the exact time to turn our heads, look into each other's eyes before closing them and pressing our lips gently to each others. It was the sweetest kiss I ever experienced and could not be compared to anything else in life. The second, third, and fourth were wonderful as well but none measured up to that first connection. It was that kiss that was the exclamation point of the evening. It was that kiss that solidified us as a couple. It was that kiss where everything made sense. That very first kiss finally answered my question. Was it love? Yes, it was.

We embarked on a world wind romance as if I had something to compare it to. This love thing was a blank slate to paint the picture of the love and life we desired. We were best friends by every definition of the word. We shared everything in extremes. All our time was spent with each other, talking to each other, supporting each other, doing for each other, or thinking about each other.

It would take another fifteen years before I would learn the parallel between establishing a natural relationship like that between "Damon" and I and a spiritual relationship between us and the Father. Just as we spend time with our love interest, gazing longingly into each other's eyes, even breathing, moving, and thinking together as one, as we establish and develop a relationship with each other so are we to do the same with Christ, the lover of our soul. As we would keep the desires, thoughts, and needs of our significant other in mind, likewise we should do the same with the creator and master of our regenerated heart?

How amazing it is that as we travel the aisles of the grocery store picking up the milk, bread, and toilet paper on our list, we will casually pass the potato chip aisle and recalling how much our sweetheart loves sour cream & onion thoughtfully we pick up a bag yet we do not conduct our day thinking whether Christ would like me to say a kind word to the stressed out secretary by the door or buy and extra sandwich at lunch for the homeless guy outside the building. Or even if He wants us to spend our time, His time, working at this particular job or if there is another assignment for our life. Perhaps Christ desires you work in a flower shop across town because that is where the suicidal man you are purposed to lead to Christ will come to buy flowers for the wife he beat the night before.

It is next to impossible to keep desires and commandments in the forefront of our mind if they are completely unknown. There must exist some measure of desire to know and fulfill God's commandments. Unfortunately not knowing due to lack of study and prayer is the position of a large portion of professed Christians. There is no personal relationship with the Savior and many who have a personal relationship struggle with the knowledge of how to successfully maintain it through an imbalance of spiritual matters and the reality of life.

Lack of knowing is not a suitable or acceptable excuse for not carrying your half of the weight or burden while yoked to Christ. We must learn. As in the days of Hosea, saints continue to die for lack of knowledge. When God's spoken and recorded commands are unknown by a born again person, they are not fulfilled. When a command is not fulfilled the offender is disobedient. Disobedience is sin. The wages of sin is still death. Hence, the saints die (become separated from God) because of sin...sin that is committed because there is no understanding of what God truly wants (lack of knowledge).

An excellent example of this is how we handle money. There is little to no knowledge among Christians of Christ's likes, dislikes, or desires concerning how we handle money. Most understand when the offering plate is passed to put something in and many yield to the 10% tithe instruction given through the years by the clergy. Today some argue that is Old Testament, yet offer no other kingdom financial principals. How to manage and use money God's way or even where to find these principles in the word continue to remain elusive. Therefore, the body continues to utilize money in ways God does not desire,(gambling, purchasing idolatrous materials, tithing but not giving offerings) cursing our household finances, keeping them separated from God thus causing a death in that area, for some saints by choice but most because we did not know.

Perhaps it is due to a lack of personal initiative or an absence of mentoring on the part of the church, it was this lack of relationship that made it so easy for me to dismiss my covenant with Christ becoming bound by and yoked to sin. Beyond maybe five or six of the Ten Commandments I had no knowledge of what God wanted for or from my life. There was little inkling of what He wanted me to say, do, or feel, and no understanding of my purpose. I did, however, know what others wanted. I did what I needed to in developing those and through sin I made the desires of other's my own. From sex to alcohol to how I spent my money, the path of the world was easy to find and travel and the anti-Christ I was yoked to was strong.

We, as a body, must step beyond just being saved into a full blown intimate relationship with Christ. This step will set our life on the path of righteousness and victory that God may be glorified through.

Often times "a yoke of sin" is preached as simply being the weight of sin on the life of the afflicted. Drug addicts are portrayed as destitute from the financial burden of their habit and homosexuals are portrayed as social deviants for their unspeakable sin. The weight of sin like the weight of a yoke is indeed a reality. However, even more so is the fact that sin yokes or binds a person to a demonic spirit. Your will is irrelevant. Through sin a person is bound to the will of one stronger then themselves.

Chapter Two

THE YOKE OF SIN

I held on to my virginity for seventeen years. The fear of my parents' wrath was at the bottom of the list of reasons to abstain. No, my primary concerns were pain and pregnancy. I played basketball so pregnancy would ruin my fantasies of a professional basketball career. I say fantasy because there was no WNBA at the time. The big time for females was college or a professional career overseas and average height chics like me were a dime a dozen. As for pain, I did not know what to expect and fifth grade sex ed. class did little for my enlightenment. Sadly, a part of me vaguely remembered some church conversation about having sex before you were married but that could not have been about me. That was for the fast girls who were just doing it to do it with no love involved. Not me and "Damon."

Whatever the reason, however, our love endured for some time without sex so I held out, enduring regular pressure from my long-time boyfriend and occasional ridicule from my friends who were all "doing it," or so they said.

There came a time during the heyday of my high school years when my relationship with my first true love began to crumble. We once shared intimate moments at the lockers between classes. There were considerations made of each other's time and feelings. Flowers, cards, and other efforts were constantly visible to express our deep commitment to the relationship and each other. Yet gradually things changed. Our love was no longer progressing and I became desperate for a way to fix what was broken. There was no love like his love and in my mind no replacement either. There was no way I could let him go.

We talked and that did not fix it. We spent quiet time together but that didn't solve the problem. Just about everything was tried to make things better but to no avail. I say "just about everything" because there was one thing I had not tried. Something my love had been asking for all along. It was something that I did not have enough information about or understanding of…sex. He "not getting any" must be why our love was falling apart. The decision was made. After all, my dedication to the relationship dictated I fulfill his desires then trust he would fulfill mine. My teenage mind rationalized this to be a small sacrifice for our greater good.

One day...that day we skipped out of school early and met at the door of my parent's home. I stood in the doorway with one hand clasping the side of the door frame and the other on my hip. As I leaned to the side offering my best bedroom eyes, my fears hampered any effort to appear sexy. After escorting him to my room I lay down and offered my body and virginity as a solution to our situation.

Shortly after our one and only teenaged love rendezvous we officially broke-up. After standing alone and vulnerable, in anticipation of the emotional return on my physical investment, I was knocked to the ground in tears with the realization my companion was no longer there. Nothing external could repair the internal damage, the cracks, and small breaks within the structure of our relationship. Sadly, my solution was not a solution at all and now it was gone. I was no longer a virgin. The purity of myself, and my body could never be given to another and I joined the legions of females who proclaimed a broken heart. A familiar sentiment entered my mind. I thought it better to have never loved him then to have met him, loved him, and have to live without him. I was devastated and soon discovered I was also naive. Little did

I know how that one act of intimacy would lead me down a destructive and life threatening road that would take years to recognize and even longer to deviate from.

The Path

The yoke used to bind cattle is not used to solely keep the animals together but is also harnessed to a plow, wagon, or other farming tools. That plow is set on a specific path which the cattle are not allowed to deviate from. It is the desired path or direction dictated by the farmer steering the plow. When we carry a yoke of sin, attached to a spirit of lying, a spirit of anger, a spirit of disobedience, or a spirit of lust as in my example, we turn the reins over to Satan to direct us down a life's path filled with destruction and lacking peace.

Light and dark cannot occupy the same space at the same time and neither can we wholly walk with both Christ and Satan allowing both wills to guide our decisions. So solely being saved does not mean we are walking according to a path designed by Christ. Loving Him and feeling Him does not mean our lifestyles exhibit a life yoked to His will. Having no relationship with Him at all will result in traveling a path through life that is walked apart from His will; His will meaning both His commandments and our assignments – the list of things we were put on this earth to do.

We can easily visualize the person completely without Christ on this barren path but this is also true for those who do know Christ. Daily we face the issues of flesh and must not take for granted how our small challenges bind us. A "little white lie" when a co-worker asks about her new hairstyle can link us to a spirit of deception. Over-indulging in shopping or food may bind us to a spirit of covetousness and gluttony. Placing the physical love of another (sex) over the spiritual love of our Savior, for example, yokes us to a spirit of lasciviousness and to Satan whose path is not that of holiness and certainly not the path desired for one who has accepted Christ as Lord.

Whether we acknowledge it or not each individual act and decision in our life has us yoked to either the will of Satan or the will of Christ. We must also remember that our will is not equal to the will of Christ simply because we are saved. Echoing Paul's sentiments, in us there is no good thing. We must continue to strive to make our thoughts and desires for our life His thoughts and desires for our life. Otherwise, like the things of Satan, what we want for ourselves will also bind us and set us on a path contrary to Christ.

Scientists will tell you there is no action without a reaction. Likewise there is no act without a consequence. That transgression or ungodly act committed – though upon repentance is forgiven by Christ – starts the individual on a path of consequences. Much like one step of an ox leads to another leading to another and another leading to the strain and fatigue of a full day of pulling, the one act of fornication by a youth seeking to understand their emotions may lead to more sexual acts to maintain the feeling, to a reputation of promiscuity, to a negative self perception, or maybe to a sexually transmitted disease, or to an unplanned pregnancy. The path of the yoked is chosen by the one who is steering.

Even acts out of our control have consequences. In ministering through drama the story of the woman at the well, I came to know a young lady barely in her twenties who after many years of sexual and physical abuse by male relatives and friends hid her femininity under baggy clothes and her sexuality through female only relationships while dulling the pain with mass quantities of marijuana and alcohol. After much conversation she revealed, "I don't want to be gay but I can't see myself being with a man." The abuse, lead to promiscuity with other abusive men, leading to a drug problem, leading her to a confused lifestyle contrary to her desires and certainly to God's will for her life. These are simply illustrations to explain how one act of sin through unknowing or direct rebellion is not simply one act of sin but rather the genesis of a path, many of which we will travel in our lifetime.

When traveling a path of habitual sin it is wonderful to know Christ is still there. His grace covers us and mercy protects us. Through sin control of the reins may have been relinquished to Satan but Christ still has ownership of the one yoked. You made an oath to Him on your day of salvation, to be bound to Him.

A Footnote on Sex

The majority of humans do not enter into this world with an understanding of God's plan for sex. As a youth that was especially true for me as sex became a tool to acquire the emotional stability and fulfillment I so craved. Unfortunately the church has been lax in taking the helm of the sexual education of our children. I do not simply refer to the teaching of abstinence but the emotional, psychological, and physiological aspects of it.

We do not offer understanding as to what occurs in the heart, mind, and body. Rather popular culture teaches human sexuality through television, music, and movies.

Celebrities become role models perpetuating casual, pre-marital lust as the norm for a healthy sex life. Body parts and social trends of bi and homosexuality are objectified and made greater than much needed emotional and spiritual development.

The message of sexual promiscuity is burned into the conscious of children before elementary school is completed. As bodies grow and natural instincts and urges are awakened, our children and youth become unbalanced in their understanding and are not equipped to keep that particular doorway of their soul guarded and closed to any unholy presence.

Sex means easy access to your spirit, corruption of your mind and heart which are components of your soul. Lust, disease, and perversions are all welcome to enter and wreck physical, emotional, and mental havoc for years after an initial sexual act, voluntary or involuntary. The sexual immaturity of our children that permit such acts to take place is rivaled only by the spiritual immaturity that leaves one virtually defenseless to the consequences.

God's plan for sex was to have man deposit a seed into a woman that it may grow and be nurtured under the protection of its mother until a time when that purpose in the form of a child can be birthed and sustain life on its own. Christ designed this for marriage to compliment the maturity and learnedness of the parents. A child cannot handle the responsibility of God's plan for sex yet their lack of education at our hands, gives them a license to misuse it. This is visible in an increase of oral sex and perverse and abusive sexual acts in the bathrooms of our children's schools, for example. Acts reported to occur as early as the third grade.

I speak of the issue of sex because I closely identify with its destructive tendencies and learned social behavior from childhood into adulthood. However, the same can be argued concerning our children's lack of preparedness in the areas of drugs, alcohol, and finances to name a few. We set parameters for when we believe our children are ready to learn what we believe to be adult lessons because we unfortunately learned them in our latter years. We even go so far as to dictate what is Kingdom related and what, like issues of sex, cannot be discussed in and by the church.

All the Earth is the Lord's and all that is in it is His. Everything is a Kingdom issue open for discussion even if the discussion is how we can redeem this corrupted thing back to Him. The result of limited and absent discussions is that we give the authority of our body and soul over to the world. We give Satan permission to occupy and control it.

We firmly place the weight of sin on our children through our inaction and voluntarily we carry it ourselves through submission to our flesh due to someone else's inaction in our own childhood and youth.

I often wonder had I known another purpose to preserve myself other than pregnancy prevention, would I have considered sex when seeking a solution to my failing young love. An answer to that question can only be glimpsed through the life of my daughter as she is afforded the opportunity to both witness Satan's plan for sex by examining the world and learn God's plan through Christian education, active parenting, and the honest testimony of her mother.

The yoke of sin we carry may have been fashioned from ignorance or simply from choosing sin as opposed to righteousness. Because we live in this world we are continually faced with the world's plan or Satan's path for our life. That path leads to destruction. When internalized, unholy tendencies become normalcy and we walk contrary to Christ, yoked, bound, and pulling the enemy's plow.

Chapter Three

RICH SOIL

I couldn't take it. I just could not take in anymore. Things never turned out the way they were supposed to. They certainly never turned out the way I wanted them to so I felt why even try? It seemed like I was fighting a losing battle, like I was pushing a rock uphill, like I was at the end of my rope and like every other ready to give up cliché known to man. I was completely fed up and felt so alone that it physically hurt. That was the life Christ rescued me from then religion retuned me to with its focus on ritual rather than relationship. Now love would have its turn to save me only to also return me to loneliness after my breakup with my high school sweetheart. I owned it. It was mine. It was depression.

A broken heart, friends and family passing, parents' divorcing and my trust and stability shaken, there was no desire to deal with the mess anymore. What mess could a young adult have? I'm glad you asked. Life – that is all I could call it and though it seemed everyone had one, I felt I was the only one experiencing one falling apart – life. No one felt or could even understand what I felt. Not my family and not my friends and definitely not my parents. They thought I was losing my mind. My father wanted me to seek "professional help." It visibly hurt him to know for the first time he could not fix one of his children's problems and there was no way to tell him how. I didn't understand it myself.

More times than not, I just wanted to lie in my bed, curled in a ball, finding security and understanding in the covers wrapped tightly around me. It felt I was getting the true hug I so desperately needed instead of the 'it's gonna be alright' pats of well meaning saints. Each disagreement with family seemed to confirm my isolation. I was alone in a house full of people. One evening the anguish after recurring sibling and parental confrontations left me uncontrollably sobbing in the corner of the bathroom floor, overwhelmed by the physical pain of my emotions. As I cried to the point of exhaustion I longed for someone to come that would make my pain go away, if only for a moment. Just long enough for me to catch my breath. Just for one moment. Easily I convinced myself no one would come. They had not up to this point. I preferred the only option certain to be effective in stopping the pain. I wanted to die.

The presence of God I felt that day I first danced in church was nowhere around. It was close enough to remember the euphoria but far enough to consider it out of reach if I considered it at all. The people I loved and could entrust with my thoughts and feelings were no longer around. The love of my life was gone, my grandmother passed, my sister moved out, my parents were separating, and my basketball idol, Len Bias, overdosed on cocaine. Practically everyone I placed my love and trust in were missing in action. Everyone else was consumed with their lives and seemingly gone from mine.

Coincidently there was something else missing; my courage. In a bathroom full of pills and straight razors my every attempt to take action was met with hesitation and incompletion. Slits of my wrists were nothing more than unsightly scratches. Each scratch and cut made the pain in my chest lessen but it did not relieve it. An effort to overdose amounted to nothing more than excessive ingestion of vitamins my body probably needed anyway and pain killers that made me sick adding to the already endless pain.

I returned to the security of my bed with the covers wrapped around me. Perhaps the desire to die would be sufficient enough to achieve the goal. In the bed was where my emotions meet. In this world of loneliness, at least I had them. They were a continual and dependable presence, like familiar friends congregating in a clubhouse. There, under my covers I could always find Doubt who was never alone. Insecurity always had a spot by her side and if I did not quite make it to the bed Loneliness would meet me at the door, keeping me company in my solitude. As I aimlessly paced around the room Fear met my exhausted and stumbling legs in a corner where I could slide to the floor finding some rest. Pain and Torment crouched down beside me keeping company with thoughts of failure and complacency. Of course there were times when I was too exhausted to hang out with any of my emotions. My tear ducts were dry, the conversations with myself all ceased, and recognizable feelings fled. I was just tired – tired and quiet. That is when I would sit in a chair with my head in my hands hoping for Numbness to overtake me.

By the time I got to the bottom of a tissue box there was usually a glimpse of understanding or a small amount of peace about whatever situation troubled me. I secretly wished someone knew what I felt. I wished someone understood the feeling of the whole world against me and all its weight on my shoulders. I tried but could not hold everything. I spent all my energy trying but the disappointing sight of each inadequately balanced weight falling piece by piece to the ground left me with no energy to hold myself up. I wonder where the energy to cry came from. I just wanted to lie there, under my covers, and be left alone.

Mercifully, that day, that first day I wanted to die would end as the assortment of pills in my belly lulled me to sleep.

Toiling the Field

While cattle or oxen are coupled and bound for their labor, the plow their yoke is harnessed to is placed on a selected path. As the cattle pull their burden the plow begins its task of toiling. It is a destructive process where the blade of the plow breaks through the ground turning the dirt to expose the fertile soil for planting.

As previously discussed, we are as one half of the oxen, upon salvation yoked to the will of Christ but through sin yoked to the will of flesh and Satan. There we carry the weight of our transgressions as opposed to the weight of purpose and divine assignments. The blade of the plow is a specific sin that opens the doorway (toiling) or in some situations literally rips a hole through your soul (ground/soil) exposing your heart (the seat of your emotions and beliefs) to begin planting new seeds of ungodly thoughts and actions. To Satan the regenerated soul of an individual who has decided to walk with Christ is good and fertile ground where he attempts to use our toiling experiences plant corruption throughout our lifetime.

As reflected in my story, after salvation fornication was the sin that toiled and turned the soil of my soul revealing my fresh, youthful, and naive soil filled with the rich emotions and beliefs of my unlearned and unprotected heart where the seeds of loneliness and depression could be planted.

There is a stage in life human behavioral scientists like to call our formative years. This is a time from our childhood into youth where specific events and particular people have a significant impact on our life. Each time one such event takes place its impact literally rips through the person we are, our beliefs, and our perceptions, and exposes our fragile and fertile soul, changing who we are. Our soul, once again is the seat of our emotions, will, and desires. It is our heart. To illustrate, a child who is friendly and helpful has a teacher who is also friendly and helpful. During preparation for a science fair the teacher spends extra quality time with the child where the child realizes they want to make students feel as special as that teacher did then matures and too becoming a friendly and helpful teacher. That time the teacher spent with that child changed who they were and influenced who they would become.

Unfortunately, not all events are positive where a teacher has influenced us into greatness. Sometimes events are negative; the death of a loved one, physical and sexual abuse suffered at home, or a broken heart. As these negative events and people tear through our soul and our heart, the soil that was meant to cultivate the word and will of God, becomes exposed and vulnerable to demonic implants.

Depression, for example, is a dangerous spirit. Yes, a spirit. Not a mental condition or a pharmaceutically treatable disease. As the effects or symptoms of depression change our flesh they are medically treatable, but they are not the source. It is a spirit – some say demon – that attacks the very soul of an individual. Once it has infested a person's toiled heart and mind, it attempts to cultivate or grow ungodly thoughts and life threatening actions. Many view depression as a downward spiral from a 'normal' life to one of despair. I offer you a contrary perspective.

As depression takes hold of an individual's lifestyle it begins to grow upward and bear fruit. Its roots are planted in activities of life and grown thick and strong in the presence of death. Happy smiling demeanors slowly transform into slight grins before growing into full-bloomed angry attitudes. Once vibrant and on the go, now 3depression grows larger than a social calendar or even a desire to get out of bed.

Linguistically and socially the word down or downward is grouped with other such perceived negatives as dark, black, and hot. If we change how we think about depression we can defeat it. The first step is the truth that it is a spirit. As important is the understanding that depression destroys through growth and does anything but decrease. The life of a depressed person may indeed feel as though it is spiraling downward when in actuality a lifestyle has been altered. It is the alterations of sleep habits, desires to socialize, and thirst for life, for example, that is the fruit boar from the ungodly seed. By recognizing a growth we recognize the ability to kill it by cutting it off at the root which is the initial sin, and closing the doorway exposing the soil or soul.

I highly recommend the book "He Came to Set the Captives Free" by Rebecca Brown. While her testimony remains controversial and challenged by some, her teaching on doorways is one of the most concise and will aid in your understanding.

Choosing to live a lifestyle of sin, or even engage in one fleshly sin of momentary pleasure opens your soul to damaging and sometimes demonic results and, as discussed in the previous chapter, sets the plow of your harnessed to your yoke on a path of destruction which can take a lifetime to deviate or recover from.

Chapter Four

FORK IN THE ROAD

High school was over and college began. With maturity came adult responsibilities. Those responsibilities included adult relationships and grown men meant business. They wanted to go out, have fun, work, and study, have intellectual conversations, and regularly feed their sexual appetite. I thought I would learn from my first sexual encounter and never put myself in the situation of having sex to keep a man again. Not so. Instead I repeated the exact same behavior hoping for a different result. That is the definition of insanity though at the time my actions felt necessary. Worse than repeating the reckless behavior was that the behavior and their consequences were completely self-imposed. Men never said "have sex or I'm gone" though the implication was there. I did, after all, date the finest brothers. Many women would have been glad to fulfill the desires of the men I dated.

I just wanted to find a brother who would make me feel loved and cherished. There were many candidates. There was "Tom" who sang to me and had the softest

55

kisses. We loved to just talk to each other. After two months of bliss the pressure was on. I figured he was my first serious sexual and personal relationship after my first encounter and the way things were going we would probably be together for years. Nope. One month later things fizzled out and were over.

Then there was "Chris." He was one of many basketball players I would find myself in this cycle with. He had his own car, a good job, and was very well focused on his future. Not to mention he treated me like a queen. We were officially a couple for several months when the heat turned up. Once again I gave him what he wanted. After all he was giving me the love, affection, and attention I wanted, right? Wrong. That lasted for about another month before he was gone. "Kenny." "Kevin." "Shawn." "Ray."

Over the years the list became long and each time the brother would give the fulfillment I so craved obligating me to express my feelings in the way he would understand. "I love you" could not express it and was probably not appropriate or honest anyway. Holding hands or giving flowers did not do the job in communicating my emotions and they wanted sex. Each time I would surrender my "expression of love" and each time our love would come to an end. Sometimes it just seemed like they hit it and split, as though there were never any true, sincere feelings for me. They were just putting in the time necessary for them to reach their goal. The emptiness and depression that followed intensified with each separation.

In addition to sex, I continued down several related paths from my past. The momentary pleasure of the scratches and cuts on my wrist from my first suicide attempt set me on a path of picking and cutting holes into my skin whenever stressed or depressed. Unsightly scars and visible scabs plagued my face and body. The practice became habit more than pleasure. The pills from the medicine cabinet that once lulled me to sleep also silently followed me. My use of pain killers became excessive resulting in excruciating stomach ulcers. Even without the ulcer, their sleepy numbing effect, while physically gratifying, became emotionally ineffective. There had to be something else that would help me stop feeling the pain of my emotions. There was.

When first introduced to alcohol it was a sincere social activity. Hanging out with my college friends and teammates, of course everyone else was drinking and drinking to get drunk. Never directly pressured to fit in, the fear of an obvious difference between me and the rest of the room and no real reason why not to was enough to influence my drinking decisions. A little fruity mixed drink in my hand would be acceptable and refreshing so I sipped on one drink for entire parties and enjoyed myself.

With each gathering came more familiarity with the friends around, so much so they became as family. Family involves a great deal of security and comfort which I needed at a time when my personal family and emotional security were falling apart. Divorce, death, repeated broken hearts, there was just loss all around me except with my friends and my drink. On those I could depend.

One slowly nursed drink then two then three. I began to learn the effects of alcohol on an individual. Not dizziness, slurred speech, or visual impairment. I learned about the ability to numb the most painful heart ache and create a desire to live consequence and judgment free. I believed this feeling could last day after day but it did not. Life went on. My new close friend would have to settle for providing an acceptable escape rather than eternal relief.

For excitement, a sorority sister and I began regularly going to the race track. It was harmless fun and cheap too at only $2 a bet. I developed a system believing that every gray or pitch black horse were guaranteed winners, especially if they wore a 6. I excelled at turning $2 into a hundred. The few times I lost were worth the cost of the adrenaline rush and excitement that came with cheering each race until the very last gallop as well as the anticipation of being the big winner amidst the crowd of expectant big winners. Instead of pain or even numbness, I had a joy that could sustain me most of the week and a medicine in alcohol to treat the symptoms on the off days. But there was still a part of me that knew something was not completely right with my behavior. After all, I was raised in the church.

Reflecting on my experience at 13 was often depressing. I could not help but wonder why God would not visit me again and make me feel the love, excitement, and energy I felt at that concert? Why wouldn't He fill me again? Why would He put me in the position to have to find in alcohol, sex, and gambling what He gave me first? Why did I have to go from one thing to another and another getting stuck in a destructive cycle? My thoughts were just another disappointment I needed to numb.

No Rest for the Weary

A yoke is made of solid wood often with iron fittings. After a period of labor a yoke becomes extremely heavy and exhausting. Each step seems to pull more and more weight. The accumulating weight of fatigue and the equipment pulling against the ground makes each effort feel insurmountable. The burden causes painful scarring and bruising around the neck and shoulders where the yoke is carried, even leaving an impression. The responsible farmer understands the signs of fatigue and gives the oxen rest and water allowing them to regain some strength and recover before continuing the process. Without such rest the animal may work themselves into dehydration, injury, and death.

The enemy seeks to kill, steal, and destroy (John 10:10) seeking to give no rest to the person who bears the burden of sin. Rest would give you an opportunity to recuperate, remember Christ, and fight. No rest. He wants you dead. Yoked to the will of Satan, the weight of one sin is added to the weight of another to the weight of another creating a spiritually exhausted soul. Rather than submitting to the will of Christ and trusting His promise in Psalm 34, that He would deliver the saints out of their many afflictions, we actively participate in the destructive process. For example, we may practice fornication and emotional dependency leading to depression leading to thoughts of suicide giving way to substance abuse and more fornication, over time each causing us to bear a greater burden than desired by God for our life and over time each leaving the scars and bruises of a damaged soul.

It is at this point where our burdens become so strenuous that we begin to question positions we constantly place ourselves in, toxins we continue to pollute our bodies with, and poisonous people whose sinful state we consistently mimic. The clubs we have such fun in become less enjoyable. The girlfriend or boo we spend our time with appear a little less interesting. The alcohol, drugs, food, shopping, sex, and religious churchy events we use to supply our joy become less fulfilling. Our purpose for all our transgressing becomes blurred leaving us no buffer from the weight of our sins and the separation from the God whose will we professed to be yoked with at our time of salvation.

Such was the case at the height of my backslidden state. Dealing with the same men and keeping up with the fun loving party façade became tedious chores with no completion or fulfillment. Like many it was at this point that I became frustrated, felt isolated, and began to breakdown from the pressure of the yoke, the labor, and the history or what I pulled behind me.

This is a similar point of desperation that led many of us from a church scene of no power and hypocrisy into the world where we believed we saw results. As results deteriorate our wounds become painfully clear and the cycle is repeated to find the next thing that will produce. It is what I deem the "Fork in the Road Syndrome." The vice runs its course and we have traveled the path leading us to the point of asking, "Which way to go."

The accumulated weight of all we are yoked to and pulling, as well as the continual toiling experience bring us to what may truly be our breaking point. This is the point we seek and are open to what to do next. Give up or get power. This is where Christ steps in.

The wonderful thing about God is that while through our lifestyle are yoked to sin, He has not abandoned the covenant we made with Him at the time of our salvation or the purpose He has for our life. He is still yoked to you underneath all those other yokes you carry and His will still reigns over the sin you pull behind you. Eventually He takes the destructive path sin places you on and causes it to collide with His will giving you another opportunity to lay down your weight and carry the yoke of Christ.

There was a moment of clarity, no matter how brief, I experienced during that time of alcohol, gambling, and sexual promiscuity. I remembered that all consuming and indescribable completeness when I danced through the church. I was clear enough to know I would have preferred that feeling over the false feeling of joy gambling gave me, or the pretend peace alcohol afforded me, or even the temporary love men provided. I knew these things but feeling powerless to achieve them I abandoned hope and gave into the world's way of manipulating my frustrations. I did not know that moment of clarity was my fork in the road.

Through that memory, God presented me with an opportunity to seek Him, find Him, and go another way. I praise God for His mercy because that was one of many missed opportunities. Like I did that day, many times when facing our fork in the road we choose to continue the path least desired for our life. I believe one reason we continue is because of that impression.

The Impression

When a man removes his baseball cap after entering a room, a line across the back of his head and sometimes his forehead become visible. This line is an impression or visual representation of the pressure of where the seam of the hat rests when it was on his the head. Likewise, the yoke we carry pulling years of sin, flesh, and transgressions, leaves more than a simple mark. It can leave an impression.

Impressions are a result of the pressure of something being left in a place over time. If you were to remove the item leaving the impression than return it at a later time, the item would fit snuggly within that impression because it recognizes its shape, size, and other characteristics. It is familiar with it. Likewise, certain sins and fleshly desires create an impression on our soul. Once that impression is made our tendency is to return to familiar things or people even if proven destructive or unproductive in the past.

This is one thought most young ladies do not consider when contemplating their first sexual experience. That experience, coupled with the pressure of emotions and desires, leave an impression in the heart and mind of the lady. In the future she will seek, accept, and return to men that fit within that impression of the initial partner. If he was skinny the attraction in adulthood is towards skinny men, dark skinned the attraction is towards dark skinned men. Even more important if he was abusive or rough the attraction is towards someone who exhibits those dominating characteristics. This is why many women find themselves saying, "Why do I always get the same type of man." It is because that is the impression of your version a desirable man on your soul (heart, mind).

You have subconsciously predisposed yourself to desiring and attracting that type of man. This is not to say a woman will not step outside that mold from time to time but through life, like the hat returning to its familiar place, so too will the woman return to a familiar type of man or woman if she begins a bi-sexual or homosexual lifestyle.

An individual will attract what they feel they deserve and are worth which is directly tied to that initial and reinforced impression. I believed my body was worth the physical sacrifice to secure relational fulfillment. I returned to that repeatedly.

The concept of an impression on the soul opens the possibility of this process affecting men as well. I would not presume to speak as an authority of how initial sexual encounters affect men but based on a spiritual understanding of how our soul absorbs our life experiences and shape our outlook, I believe a similar outcome exists for men also.

This discussion serves well to illustrate why when faced with a divine opportunity to abandon our sinful lifestyle we choose to continue down a sinful path. Likewise, if we returned to Christ it explains our secret desires and continued pull back to our unholy lifestyle. You sat our mess so long and allowed the pressure to dig a deeper and deeper impression into your soul. When presented with a spiritual decision – to return and follow Christ – we depend on our learned understanding and make a natural choice to continue on the path that is familiar, comfortable and in many cases easier than working to remain in right standing with Him.

Ironically, as it has happened repeatedly in the past, the familiar path we choose ends in unfulfilling frustration. Little do we know this frustration and desperation is the beginning of God chastening us back toward His will and His purpose for our life. It takes us full circle back to the fork in the road where we can choose to return to a walk with Him.

Chapter Five

CHASTENED

I loved that feeling. I loved the feeling of numbness, of joy, and of emotional fulfillment. It was not the alcohol, sex, or gambling. It was the feeling but that coveted feeling started to lose its effect. I mean, I began to hurt more when not drinking making me want to drink more. I was lonelier after my latest encounter which made me want to feel an embrace again. There was no excitement when not gambling that I had to play more and more just to not feel the pain...but I still did.

I was less fulfilled with each effort. Not only had the payoff diminished but the reality of the consequences began to take hold. I became dependent on alcohol to relax and function through the chaotic life of an out of control graduate student. That dependency left me forging unhealthy relationships with individuals I knew could supply my addiction.

In efforts to ease the loneliness and low self worth I sought the security of men and allowed them to fulfill many of their desires at the expense of my body and soul. At the time the momentary gratification was worth any risks. These were voluntary risks and perceived necessities that both threatened my life and helped to save it by giving something to cling to rather than the desire of death.

I could find completion and fulfillment in nothing and the tools that once gave me pleasure quickly became liabilities. My $2 bets at the local racetrack became $20 bets. If there was indescribable excitement at $2, surely more money meant more joy. That logic proved flawed. More money meant more anxiety. I suppose that feeling may have been different if the winning streak from the smaller wages continued with the larger ones but no such luck. That is, after all, what I was depending on…luck. Luck, I know now, is completely different than favor. Today I understand favor will make things happen when everything around me says it should not. Luck couldn't produce the monthly rent payment that I regularly gambled away.

As my happiness deteriorated and I begin to re-evaluate the effectiveness of my emotional fillers, it occurred to me to return to another familiar source of happiness. Why was I searching for a man to make me feel the way my first love made me feel? Why was I trying to recapture the overwhelming excitement of spiritual and emotional completion through unclean spirits when I could find a way to reconnect with my original source? The decision was made, I needed to look for the love of my life and return to where I thought Christ was. I needed to return to church and get back with "Damon". Fortunately neither took long.

My high school sweetheart was ready for love also. He thought of me in North Carolina while I sat in an apartment in Milwaukee thinking of him. He returned home to Maryland and on one of my routine trips there from school, we re-kindled our romance. After my graduation we quickly married. Having been raised in the church I knew the road back to Christ. I would just find a church to call home and attend regularly. Everything I saw and was taught told me that was the way to Christ. If you were not in church you were bad and if you were in church and did that confession at the altar you were saved.

By making a commitment to both my God and my new husband, I was making a commitment to not pursue what I once pursued as a result of straying from both. There would be no participating in promiscuity nor would I fill my body with unclean substances. There was no reason to do any of that now anyway. My body was the temple of God and my marriage would be an example of what I understood holiness to be. But things were not so cut and dry when it came to gambling.

No one could give me any scriptural reason why I should not gamble, in any form; horses, greyhounds, or lotto. I mean, the stock market is a form of chance and gambling and the "money now" and "prosperity today" movements of the church preached engaging in such activities to better your financial status and leave a legacy for your children. Our Pastors had become examples of how prosperous you can be when you utilize the stock market as part of your personal money management. Someone mentioned also having faith and trusting in God to provide a Kingdom answer. A thought like that is useless to someone with a gambling issue. "I am trusting in Him to provide me with the right numbers or make my horse come in," was a regular response.

I had a form of faith in His provisions but saw no fruit. My husband found finding a well paying IT job without a college degree difficult to say the least. And to the surprise of most, the salary of a fulltime gospel radio personality was two steps below public school teacher. Most believe those in entertainment with a name and a bit of popularity are "living large" but as newlyweds we were regularly strapped for money and living paycheck to paycheck.

Even more discouraging was the seeming effect my past promiscuity had on my intimacy with my husband. Emotionally draining relationship after emotionally draining relationship left me conditioned to believe in sacrificing my desires and myself in an effort to keep the man that my love and life revolved around. I was detached from the true man I married and attached to a false belief of what he as a man wanted. I could not present to him the true woman he married for the compulsive need to give what I believed was required. Furthermore, the health issues I incurred from my promiscuous lifestyle left devastating damage to my body and threatened my possibilities of motherhood. For a period of our marriage, the emotional and physical pain of the past made intimacy challenging.

All this and still there had been no visitation from the power that excited me some thirteen years prior. I fulfilled my commitment and joined a church, knew my Pastor, and attended service regularly yet felt nothing. I felt nothing but the intense frustration, confusion, and emptiness that plagued my life. This time it seemed the intensity of these most depressing and oppressing emotions increased as I escalated in new levels of my adult life.

The Chastening of God

Chastening is God's process of correction for the purpose of removing the yoke, bondage, and burden of sin from your life to foster relationship and fulfill purpose. Though it often feels like it, chastening is not His anger or wrath toward us. However, it is possibly one of the most painful places to be in Christ. How can you still be in Christ if you are living an active life of sin and have strayed so far from His commandments? To first deal with the question of sin, "all have sinned and fallen short of the glory of God (Rom 3:23)" therefore lack of sin cannot be the sole requirement for being "in Christ."

Simply put, having accepted Christ as your personal Lord and Savior makes you a part of the family. He is Father and you are son and you cannot change that. The purpose for your new life is to give Him glory in everything you do including sharing the gospel of His death, resurrection, and ascension for the winning of souls.

It is those in the body – His sons and daughters – who He loves and cares to correct. He takes the time to orchestrate opportunities that place us back on track to fulfill His purpose. This sentiment is repeated throughout the scriptures. From the Old Testament where Solomon advices in Proverbs 3:11-12;

"My son, do not despise the chastening of the Lord,

Nor detest His correction;

For whom the Lord loves He corrects,

Just as a father the son in whom he delights."

To the New Testament where it is decreed in Hebrews 12:7;

"If you endure chastening, God deals with you as with sons; for what son is there whom a father does not chasten?"

God desires for us to live our life in accordance with the covenant we made when we stood before Him, privately or publicly, and requested the use of His blood to wash our sins clean and He enter our heart. He desires that we fulfill our end of the commitment we made to live according to His will for our life. I believe that Christ understands from His experience as a man, that our flesh has more experience being fleshly than our heart does living holy, resulting in daily struggles to fight against internalizing images, music, places, and people that might cause us to fall back into a lifestyle resembling a pre-washed soul. In other words, I believe He understands it is easier for our mouth to say "we are in this world and not of this world" than it is for our flesh to walk it out.

When it is all said and done Christ must get the glory out of our life. That is why He uses the situations we experience when in a state of living contrary to His will to help another.

Our frustrations over a particular area, our anger at a certain state of affairs, our resolution to a specific societal ill is most certainly a set up for ministry birthed from our own past rebellion. If you are tired of participating in the worldly routine of the singles scene Christ may be calling you to the area of effective singles ministry. Frustrated with seeing young men hanging on the same corner you once frequented, poorly dressed with no visible efforts of ensuring their future? You may be called to open a male mentoring program for the betterment of your Jerusalem or immediate neighborhood. If you have wondered why young sisters in the church are still becoming pregnant before they graduate high school twenty years after your same experience, possibly it is due to the young women's ministry dormant inside you.

Please note, ministry means to meet a need. It does not mean to preach, or open a church, or run a church auxiliary. It means to meet a need something we have all been called to do and He often uses our past mess to ensure we are effective.

Yes, He uses our passions as well as our experiences. Rape victims become counselors and advocates for legislative change. Even the most destructive of life's experiences must work together for our good and are turned for His glory in the Earth. Saul was most passionate about killing Christians. With all the bloodshed he caused the energy of his passion and wisdom of his experiences was harnessed by Christ helping converted Paul to become perhaps the greatest voice of the New Testament.

Christ calls each of us to a personal ministry for the betterment of the kingdom utilizing the reality of our sinful past but under His grace and protection. It is our purpose.

Pulling us toward discovering and completing our divine purpose is part of the chastening process and possibly the part we fight the most. In addition to sins of lust, over-indulgence, lying and the like, we are corrected from our disobedience toward this directive of ministry or meeting a need. Unfortunately we will more readily submit to returning to a holy lifestyle before we will agree to expose our past to help others or for the salvation of those still in the world. Christ chastens us and calls us back to Him for a reason greater than placing another notch in His soul's won belt. He has to get the glory out of our life. He has to show through you that despite everything, He is still God. He sacrificed Himself so we would have the opportunity to give Him that.

Chapter Six

IT'S ABOUT RELATIONSHIP

Life seemed to finally produce and God seemed to finally forgive everything of my past. All the obvious sins, some seemingly bigger than others, felt washed away and my new life began; literally. After a number of procedures and a major surgery to correct the damage promiscuity caused, I became pregnant and gave birth to my new joy, my new reason to live; my daughter. Just in time for that miracle we were able to move to a larger apartment in a more peaceful neighborhood. My husband found a better paying job and finally I began receiving a salary and making pretty good money on the side hosting gospel concerts and various Christian events.

With definite money to pay the monthly bills we were able to fully line up with God and tithe regularly. Everyone seemed to preach about prosperity and how financial freedom depended on giving back to the kingdom of Christ. "Without giving and tithing, your money will be cursed," clergy commanded. We fully accepted that and did our best to adhere to it. Still, no one could explain to me why gambling was wrong…so I continued. Rarely, but occasionally I would visit the local racetrack, however, lottery tickets began to interest me greatly and were more convenient.

Life was good. I had a husband that loved me, a daughter who looked just like me, and I was steadily advancing in the gospel radio industry. The only void I felt was spiritually. As a family we were starving for something more from God. There was decreasing interest in church as usual and eventually completely no desire to fellowship at all. Excuse after excuse was made for staying home this Sunday then the next and the next. Finally, in an effort to maintain a professional relationship I accepted a friend's invitation and reluctantly dragged my family to a church clear on the other side of the county.

At first it appeared to be just another one of the many store front churches popping up in Prince George's County, Maryland. It was a big store but it was still a store. Certain there would be no power there either we dipped in the back and waited for the close of service to reveal our attendance but I underestimated the offering. That is where I was exposed. As we marched to the front of the church with our offering there she stood, second row from the front, saving 3 seats just for us. All efforts to assure her we were satisfied in the back were dismissed as we were ushered to the front in "special guest" status.

The Pastor took his pastoral place in front of the church to begin his message. There was something obviously different about this church and this Pastor though I could not pin point what. With a 15-month old jumping and screaming at my feet it was hard to focus and figure it out. My husband retreated from the sanctuary with our daughter and things became clearer.

I was always partial to medium size churches. There you get a chance to truly learn who you are fellowshipping with. This medium sized church seemed to be filled with people like me. From the Pastor to the Ushers, all around me were people hungry for more. As though spiritually starved to malnourishment, these sought understanding in His word and a glimpse of His glorious presence with a fervor I had never seen collectively but certainly craved personally. All this was done with such honesty and warming comfort that it was inviting. I had a wonderful experience and by the conclusion of the altar call I had finally experienced another encounter with God. As tears streamed down my face there was a spiritual embrace that helped to restore my belief in His presence. Convinced this was the place He was visiting I knew this was where I had to be. My husband agreed and we joined the next week.

Yes, life was getting better and it was also changing. A new spiritual home and a new covering opened the door to tremendous revelation and a new found relationship with Christ. Up to this point I had no clue this whole "saved" thing was supposed to be about a relationship with Christ, learning His likes, dislikes, and seeking to please Him rather than the ritualistic routine organized religion taught. Many years after meeting Him I began to grow in Him and feel His presence regularly, even graduating to hearing His voice, a concept that had been of unending confusion to me.

Perhaps the greatest change was in my perspective of things I continued to do. I reconsidered personal acts I believed to be okay even after re-dedicating my life to Christ. Those included gossiping, judging, and of course gambling. I became uncomfortable in my actions but still had no scriptural explanation of how playing the lotto was a sin. Soon that point proved useless.

One Monday, the day after hosting a packed gospel concert at the region's largest church, I stopped by the grocery store for a few things decided to also get a few quick pick lotto tickets. "The jackpot is getting big so I must get in on this," I tried to convince myself. As I walked out with tickets and change in hand I passed a sister entering the store. She looked into my face with a smile that said she recognized me. Was she at the concert last night? Did she know me from another church? Did she listen to my radio show? I did not know and nothing past a friendly "hello" was exchanged before the peaceful look of familiarity soured to a look of disappointment and disgust.

She saw the tickets. Suddenly the same questions emerged. Was she someone who saw me at the concert last night? Did she see me at another church? Did she listen to my show? The same questions with different motives…did she recognize me and now view me as just another person talking the talk but not walking the walk? I had a great dislike for hypocritical people and Ministers like that. I came across them regularly in my line of work and it disgusted me. Perhaps that is why I recognized the woman's unsatisfied look. It was the same look I gave gospel recording artists that were undercover homosexuals and world renowned Bishops that offered me their hotel key.

I was so embarrassed. I literally felt dirty from the guilt and then came the most depressing thought – Christ must be as disappointed in me as I.

God Needs Your Attention

Most people will admit that during periods of sin or backsliding there were times of much fun. We enjoyed drinking, or smoking, or fornicating and were probably pretty good at it. However, there came memorable events that helped the appeal of our actions lose their luster. Things stopped working the way they once worked. In actuality, things were working exactly how they were designed to work. The things of this world or the things we can see, touch, and use for our desires, are temporary (2 Corinthians 4:18). Though their hollowness persists, we typically miss God's initial warning signs until His blatant hand of correction spiritually slaps us awake.

That is certainly what happened in my case with gambling. The excitement I once craved was replaced by a habit of purchasing tickets for chance. The act increasingly became uncomfortable yet I continued to indulge as an arrogant statement to "church folk" who could not adequately prove my act was sin. The discomfort did not deter me. The developing paranoia that someone would recognize me and misconstrue my motives could not curve my behavior. I missed every polite tap on the shoulder Christ gave me to turn from my actions and seek an understanding of financial stewardship in Him. He loved me so that He orchestrated a scene in the middle of a grocery store parking lot to humble me, correct me, and draw me to submit to His will.

In this case it was His will that I trust Him and depend on Him for my needs and understanding. The gambling was a physical manifestation of the spiritual abandonment of my dedication to Christ. When our focus is on something other than Christ that thing is made greater. It does not matter if it is a drug, a person, or a job. When we take our eyes off Christ and look to the little god in our life to fulfill our needs and desires, we have replaced the Christ we have yoked ourselves to. The Father will not allow His son to remain in such a state without correcting him/her. This is what chastening is about.

Sometimes God has to get us to a point where we are stripped of all the ungodliness that is us. Our out of control behavior must be subdued so we can submit and our attitude has to be humbled. All this sounds punishing. I assure you, God's chastening expands outside our borders of understanding concerning punishment. Scriptures give us specific consequences for our sin, so punishment is indeed a part but there is more. When God is chastening us to humble ourselves that we may return to Him and re-dedicate our life to His will and way, two things cease to take place; (1) God stops protecting us and (2) God stops intervening for us. These sound harsh for the loving Father we know. Your challenge in accepting this will be directly related to your understanding of grace and mercy but indeed both occur.

The person who has issues managing money and regularly depends on that friend to bail them out may suddenly find their reliable friend unwilling to meet their needs. An individual who found frequent social enjoyment of illegal drugs without incident cannot comprehend the recent life threatening violence they endure as a result of their habit. The one who found security in years of disease free promiscuity find themselves questioning their decisions as repeated tests return positive.

In the case of my defiant gambling, I found myself exposed as a hypocritical representative of the gospel. God could have diverted the attention of the woman or urged me to cover the tickets as I usually did, but He chose then to not intervene in the unfolding events nor protect me from the painful consequences.

In most cases it has only been the grace of God that has kept saints from financial ruins, a drug overdose, AIDS, STDs, or public humiliation. When God stops protecting us from the consequences of our actions and stops intervening in potentially harmful situations, He is seeking to correct us through revealing life as it would truly be without Him. At this point we are sons of God. We are saved and have accepted Him as our Lord and Savior so we are expected to live our lives with Christ as the head. Through sin that ceases to occur and we become separated from God. He does not desire that yet during the chastening process we experience, first hand, life if Christ where to step out and leave us with our issues.

Fortunately, since His primary purpose is correction God never completely leaves us. His withdrawal is orchestrated to the degree the individual can survive with a testimony that Christ can get the glory from. That takes us back to ministry. He does not seek to turn you over to the one who would destroy you. That is reserved for those who are not sons or even for those sons that blatantly refuse to adhere to His correction.

During this difficult period you have to stay focused and know He only wants to bring you back in line with His will for your life and a declaration of re-dedication does not help one transcend this season quicker. Christ knows our hearts and knows when there is residue of sin that can further distract us from Him. He will chasten us until every ounce of what we see, don't see, and will not admit too is bought in line. The yoke of a particular sin must be completely shattered and broken beyond repair.

Chapter Seven

GETTING TO KNOW HIM

I was free. Finally, after years of being tied to so much weight I was free. The burden of maintaining the desires of my flesh had been lifted. No longer would I be worried about someone seeing me purchasing lotto tickets. I had no concern that an innocent trip to a corner store for money orders would spark a taste to consume alcohol. Yes, the weight was gone. The taste was gone. In its place was the responsibility and renewed desire to maintain the personal relationship I had developed with Christ.

My sole desire in life was to please Him. I so wanted Him to be pleased with my marriage, while raising my daughter, and especially with the radio ministry He trusted me with. My career had advanced to a national voice to more than 2 million listeners on XM Satellite Radio and DirectTV, as well as a Sunday morning FM position on one of the top Urban stations in Washington, DC. The latter was priority for me. My local listeners increased from several thousand to several hundred thousand in a matter of weeks. The responsibility to ministry was great. Many were listening on their way from a night at the club or on their way to work or while traveling through the area on their way home from a long weekend. In each scenario, the only exposure to Jesus for that day and possibly the week would be through the music and messages I presented.

I took the opportunity very seriously and was determined to be successful so God could be glorified and selfishly, so God would be proud of me. He, after all, knew better than anyone where I came from.

To meet the primary goal of pleasing Him I needed to know what exactly made Him happy. My husband and I knew each other for fifteen years before we married and were fairly familiar with each other's likes and dislikes. Sadly, I knew Christ as long and was clueless of His desires outside of maybe five of the Ten Commandments. The work to develop a personal relationship with Christ would be a process similar to getting to know my husband and would require great dedication on my part.

Through much prayer we would need to have honest and frequent conversations to see what the concerns of the relationship were. Absent were the moaning and rhythmic petitions familiar in the Pentecostal church. As the song said, I just "had a little talk with Jesus" as I would any friend or confidant.

Daily I made the time to speak with Him and quickly He spoke back. That was one of my greatest questions after receiving Christ. How do you know when God is talking to you? The best response came from my sister who advised the experience was much like the closeness of best friends who know each other's thoughts, can finish each other's sentences, and can recognize their voice and laughter from the other side of a crowded room. Over time that type of closeness developed and I could distinguish His communication from my own thoughts.

Many of our conversations were focused on my spiritual betterment as well as an understanding of issues I bought before Him. For a basic foundation and understanding of what Christ commands of me and His promises to me I needed to seek His word. That required serious hours of personal bible study. To be successful the same discipline it took to complete graduate school would need to be applied to this task and all I learned would need application in my everyday life.

Constant prayer, staying consistent with daily readings, consciously choosing to deny what I wanted for the wants of Christ, and making meeting needs a priority was a heavy burden to carry and maintain. It was similar but not exactly the same burden as the weight attached to the life of a promiscuous gambling alcoholic.

Life was just as busy and I exerted the same commitment and energy to maintaining the life of a son out of His will as I now did the life of a dedicated Christian. But there was still something different. Maybe it was my state of spiritual innocence or perhaps my thirst for more of His presence. Perhaps it was my vigor to learn or my desire to please Christ. Whatever it was, "it" made the work simple and the responsibility easy to bear.

The Yoke of Righteousness

Now that the yoke of sin and Satan has been removed and God has chastened us, the decision to re-commit our lives to Christ means we once again are yoked. In this renewed state we are yoked to the will of the Father with Christ at the reins guiding and directing rather than yoked to the will of flesh with Satan or our own desires at the reins.

There is a difference in the yoke of righteousness and the yoke of sin. Life's experiences in the world have exposed characteristics of the yoke of sin that will help you identify it. Among them are pressure, heaviness, anxiety, and stress. Satan's yoke keeps an individual oppressed and bound to their transgressions the weight of which causes, among many things, spiritual fatigue. Just maintaining a habit can wear a person out. Staying in ungodly relationships with toxic people can destroy our body. Life becomes chaotic and fleshly desires serve as a distraction from anything of God. This is a fair description of life when yoked to the will of Satan which is sin.

Galatians 5:1 says

"Stand fast therefore in the liberty by which Christ has made us free, and do not be entangled again with a yoke of bondage."

This scripture clearly describes the yoke we are freed from through salvation as "bondage." It is as something that can "entangle" or tie up and oppress areas of our life and freedom from such through Christ is described as "liberty." This example also gives us a look at the characteristics of a yoke of righteousness.

When yoked to sin we practice a life of pleasure and desires of the world. When yoked to Christ and in right-standing we follow the commandments of Christ as dictated to us through scripture and personal relationship. Similarly to the yoke of sin there is a dedication to daily implementation but this yoke partners us to God's will for our life. 1 John 5:3 reads:

"For this is the love of God, that we keep His commandments.
And His commandments are not burdensome."

Though the sacrifice of offering and consistent tithing is similar to the sacrifice of our paycheck to drugs or alcohol the task is not troublesome. Though we give hours and days of our time to fellowship with like-minded Christians similar to when we partied with friends in the clubs until the sun rose, the duty is not grueling. Though the dedication of emotions and energy to satisfying the pleasures of the Spirit are similar to the dedication of fulfilling pleasures of the body, the responsibility is not weighty.

When in the world we often view the "saved" life as completely void of freedom but rather full of rules and regulations for how we must live our lives. They are rules that hold us from the fun of the world when in actuality it is the fun of the world that is the weight and Christ that is the freedom.

After returning to a relationship with Christ I found myself overly zealous to serve believing that was an outward representation of my right standing (righteousness) and my closeness to Him. I was at every service, bible study, weekly prayer, and multiple auxiliary meetings. I found myself at church a minimum three to four nights a week with very little rest, personal or family time. Pleasing Him became an exhausting chore and the pride of presentation became a weight until He returned me to Matthew 11:29-30.

"Take My yoke upon you and learn from Me, for I am gentle and lowly in heart, and you will find rest for your souls. For My yoke is easy and My burden is light."

Serving Him should not be so daunting. In His words the burden of service and ministry should be "light." Our relationship had been about me and how I wanted to please Him as opposed to how He desired to be pleased. Even with good intentions the weight of my selfishness was as heavy as a cocaine habit.

This scripture is also a clear directive from Jesus himself that we let go of Satan's yoke which partners us with sin and pick up His yoke partnering us with His commandments; among them having no other gods before Him. Only through walking joined with Christ will the torment within us drawing us to promiscuity, drugs, or over-eating (for example) cease and our soul find restful peace in thoughts of His grace, His mercy, and eternity with Him. We must let go of the heavy burdens that through His blood we have been freed from and pick up the light burden of righteousness.

Chapter Eight

NOT THIS AGAIN

There were many opportunities to reflect on my reconnected relationship with Him. It began to feel like much of what should work for me worked against me. Attacks to my health were a regular occurrence with everything from migraines to fatigue induced system wide shutdown to full-fledged medical procedures. Family who professed salvation was less than supportive of my new stand for righteousness as it altered my opinion of their lifestyle. And difficulties continued to plague my young marriage and threaten divorce. With all the drama I had to wonder what happened to the spiritual honeymoon I was on with my Savior.

There was a vitality in me fueled by my renewed commitment that I thought was mutual. Though "getting saved" at 13 did not do it, surely my <u>return</u> to Christ would mark the end of my suffering and challenges. That was among the promises I discovered in His word. I could quote like clichés how as a righteous one He would never leave or forsake me and He'd make my enemies my footstool but situation after situation I felt more and more alone, forsaken, and encircled by my waiting enemies.

It was obvious my timing was not the same as God and getting an understanding from Him was increasingly difficult. I returned to Him and dedicated my life to doing what He wanted. Lord, what had I done to deserve feeling this way? Angry...isolated...and alone...why do I have to feel this familiar way? It was the way I felt when in the world. I know questioning God was not the smartest thing to do but He was the only one with the answers.

Most Pastors were still preaching prosperity in the 90's. "Money is looking for you." It was not looking very hard because I was right here once again increasingly challenged by financial issues. "You're on the verge of your breakthrough!" That has been going on a minute too. How long must I be on the verge and why can't I just breakthrough? I longed for some positive familiarity other than the negativity I was feeling.

Once again, I felt apart from Christ. During the most difficult times my mind wanted me to retreat to the safety of the world I left. It did not seem to not matter that I left several years ago. The sights, sounds, and smells were again right before me without actually being there. After several days of intense arguing with my husband and it looked as though there was no drop of hope to squeeze out, I went out with some sorority sisters for some separation time. I had not been out with this crowd for quite a while as my commitment to Christ and work took precedence over any activities of the organization but this night I needed to clear my head.

Completely oblivious to the struggles of my marriage, no one could have known an innocent evening at a restaurant would take me from my body and return me to the comfort of my past drunken state. I inhaled deeply the strong smells emanating from the bar. I could taste on my tongue alcohol's tingling sensation and felt its gentle burning soar down my throat then embraced its numbing power…and I never drank a drop. I never drank a drop but felt it all in me and wanted it so bad so once again the pain would end.

When my senses sobered from my emotionally induced intoxication I felt as filthy as the first day my eyes were opened to my issue. Guilt soon followed. I was to be an example of righteousness to others and a soul for the Father to be proud of. How can this be? The word sorry is not sufficiently descriptive to express how I felt before Him; guilty and once again exposed. Fear too took its place in my mind. I worried will problems in my marriage or life, frustrate me until one day I accept the proposition of another? If I fall short of money tomorrow will I take my chances at the track? Is all that still in me too? I thought I was delivered. I thought with all that is in me, I could resist temptation. I returned to the will of God and made a concerted effort to resist the flesh and will of the world. Everything in me desired to be closer to Christ. Even in the midst of trial I prayed fervently, fasted regularly, and searched His word for a response. My heart desired Him. So how could I still want that?

Life After Chastening

The chastening process does not end the second we decide to re-commit to Christ or His will. The children of Israel walked in the wilderness for 40 years. They were not just being punished by God for their idolatry but the new generation was being chastened out of the sin of their fathers into a place ordained by God. In Joshua 5:2-9 God commanded Joshua to circumcise all the men of the new generation. Grown men, 40 and under were circumcised as a symbol of their covenant with God but upon their re-dedication there still was not an immediate national movement into the promised land flowing with milk and honey. There was an adjustment period marked by a time of healing. Their physical healing was, likewise a symbol the spiritual healing and regeneration taking place. Though the kingdom practice of the physical mutilation made circumcision bearable (His burden is light) it made the reality of it no less painful.

There is always some pain and discomfort associated with the cutting away of flesh. Israel cut away physical flesh by circumcising, and we cut away our fleshy desires by removing those weaknesses from our life. There will be a period upon our return to Christ where we feel the separation pain of what we knew for so long. There is also a separation of who we knew, not just the friends we transgressed with but with the person we were. Leaving long-time friends, even perceived sisters and brothers in the desperate state we abandoned is painful. We so want them to feel the same freedom salvation has given to us. Many saints feel this area of separation so greatly they wreak havoc in their own life believing it their responsibility to save those they left behind.

This period of painful adjustment happens when we return to a committed relationship with Christ after years of disobedience and sin, and is a period rarely spoken of in the church. The belief that saved folk have "the joy of the

Lord" and therefore have no problems continues to be perpetuated and the pressure to conform often leaves saints feeling cornered when challenged by their emotions and resurfacing desires. It can confuse new or re-dedicated saints when they are torn between the ideology of the perfect Christian and the reality of self and real-life issues. Some souls return to the world or compromise as the pressure of religion becomes too great. Many become frustrated with trying to meet the standard set by others rather than leaning to their relationship with Christ. Then there are those leaders and clergy who damage the integrity of the faith with a massive public fall from grace as their religion is shown brighter than their humanity.

After the men's foreskin healed following circumcision they had to fight several battles before entering into the promise land. Seemingly negative situations, as in our chastening period, are orchestrated by God as a part of our spiritual training. Success in maintaining right standing with Christ is a continual battle fought on the battleground of our soul. At stake are the emotions, beliefs, and values that were corrupted for so long but are redeemed once again.

In a military boot camp, during training new recruits learn more of themselves and how they respond to conflict, they get to know the persons they fight with, and they learn the enemy's tactics. Similarly, the spiritual training chastening and the yoke of Christ introduces us to, teaches how we operate, how God operates, and how the enemy operates. It shows us who we are, who God is, and who the enemy or Satan is. This training serves to expose, acclimate, and re-introduce us to the body of Christ. Much like the men of Israel could not return to the camps until their circumcised genitalia were healed, God seeks to expose and expel all the greasy residue of our past that may cause us to once again slip into sin or contaminate another son. Also, He seeks to show to us the remaining areas of our life we have not fully committed to Him.

Would the stress of a failing relationship and a hostile work environment cause you to desire the numbing escape alcohol once provided? In the midst of conflict could you taste its very tingling sensation on your tongue? Would that taste and that stress out-weigh your trust in God to fulfill His promises to you? Are any such thoughts from the enemy or are your personal lusts? If an opportunity presented itself to momentarily return to sin would you accept with the belief that God would once again forgive? Is Christ truly your life's focus or are there still issues within your flesh that have yet to be resolved? Good intentions would dictate the answers are 'certainly not' but one cannot honestly know until divinely tested with such situations.

God has the unique position of knowing our hearts. While we are proclaiming "no, no, no Christ, I will never go back to that," He can see if deliverance has truly taken place or if we are willing to transgress by thought or action. Furthermore, like the scars on the neck of previously yoked oxen, He can see the spiritual scars left from a damaging past and in His omnipotence knows the acts those wounds may pull us back to. He trains us to learn of Him so we can effectively execute His plan for our life without "us" getting in the way.

Hebrews 12:11 reads

"Now no chastening seems to be joyful for the present, but painful; nevertheless, afterward it yields the peaceable fruit of righteousness to those who have been trained by it."

Our training allows us to steadily carry the yoke of Christ we have chosen for our life that we might maintain a holy lifestyle and effective personal ministry. Thus the seed planted at salvation in our toiled heart will bear godly fruit.

Chapter Nine

UNYOKED

Living a life yoked to righteousness as opposed to yoked to sin is a daily choice and challenge. The cycle of living a lifestyle of rebellion, surviving through the process of God's chastening into a return to covenant may be repeated numerous times in one person's lifetime with each completion elevating that person to their next level of understanding in Christ. That elevation is contingent on the full completion of each cycle.

Throughout my life's story, as depicted in these chapters, I chose to give up one thing only to replace it with something more vile, addictive, and damaging then the first. Many would appropriately apply Matthew 12:43-45 to my situation believing when the initial sin was removed it came back along with seven more demons greater than itself. However, there is more to it than that. When the yoke of sin was removed from my neck there was nothing Godly to replace it with. The cycle was not completed.

Of course even in the deepest depths of my sin Christ was hidden in my heart; I was after all saved.

Occasionally He shined long enough for me to get my head above the demon infested water and breathe His holy air. Maybe it was a good sermon at Easter that got to me or one of the times I began to pray for help during a crisis becoming guilty of proclaiming the familiar sinner's promise, "If you get me out of this, Lord I will never go back to that and I promise to serve you."

The problem was and is for many, that when we believe a yoke is removed it is more accurately laid down and replaced with self as opposed to being completely destroyed and replaced with the righteousness of Christ. The latter would be the completion of the cycle. After my initial experience early in life I laid down fornication because I did not want to get pregnant. Not because my body was a temple where Christ was forced to dwell in the midst of my mess. Not because I knew pre-marital sex was not the will of Christ. Not because my parents would not approved and not because I already experienced a broken heart. I briefly stopped because my desire was to not have the responsibility of a child and my immediate future plans included college not motherhood. The sole determining factor of my abstinence was self. Even if I thought of what my parents would think or how people in the church would view me differently, the incentive was to please and represent me, not Christ. Therefore, when the doorway to fornication was re-opened that spirit of lust returned with full force, bringing with it sickness, emotional torment, abuse and a few more of its demon buddies.

This process is far more devastating for persons who do not know Christ. They believe there is only themselves to factor into their life's equations. We have the will of Christ to not just consider but focus on. That is why the chastening of God is so important to the cycle. Unique to our situations it is something we should treasure as His tool to correct, re-focus, and draw us closer to Him. His chastening gives us the infallible and indisputable purpose behind our choice to release sin from our life. The rationale behind abstinence would no longer be "because I don't want to get pregnant" but rather "Christ has a will assigned to my single, childless life." The reasoning for no longer abusing prescription drugs would not be "I can't afford the habit anymore" but rather "my body is the temple of Christ and is not mine to pollute." A depressed person would decide to get out of the bed not because "I'm tired of my mom bugging me to get out the house" but rather "because the joy of the Lord is my strength."

God's chastening reminds us of the commitment we made at salvation or re-dedication to His will and to His commandments for our life. It causes the sin-filled saint to consider the prospect of a natural life without Him, His promises and His benefits. More importantly, it is the process that gives us insight about our unrighteous lifestyle and exposes the thorns of our flesh – those ungodly things we continue to have a tendency to secretly desire even after choosing to cease actively participating.

Christ will continue to chasten and expose areas of our flesh as our spiritual maturity and promotion in Him dictates. Correcting my alcohol addicted, fornicating, gambling ways was God's first step in re-dedicating me to Him. It was what needed to be addressed for that level of my spiritual maturity. As I grew in Christ, advanced in an understanding of His word and elevated in ministry, it became necessary for Him to chasten other areas of my flesh. He exposed trust issues, judging propensities, and gossiping tendencies I had and corrected them so I could progress. As Christ enlarged my radio ministry and I became increasingly recognizable in public, it became necessary for Him to chasten the area of presentation. A servant of the most High God needed to represent Him in a spirit of excellence.

Some may say the way you dress is not a sin any more than a lack of trust in others or gossiping. They may not be in our category of "the big sins" but they are issues of self and flesh and it is our fleshly desires that separate us from Christ. He chastens us from those desires that we might be closer to Him without walls or filters. In a broad sense, anything that separates us from Christ is sin. So while I would have preferred to always present myself with an afro, jeans and a t-shirt, God had to correct my perception of presentation so I could once again advance in His will for my life. This process will continue to repeat throughout my life and the lives of others as God seeks to remove the distractions and pieces of flesh that hinder His will we are yoked to.

Lastly, our covenant with Christ must be a lifestyle and not simply individual actions. It is not something to consider solely when an overt opportunity to sin presents itself in our personal life. It is the way we are to conduct ourselves every minute of every hour of everyday. It is a lifestyle and daily fulfillment means the successful destruction of individual yokes of sin.

When yoked to the will of the world we integrated sin in every facet of our life. When at work we thought about the atmosphere of the party we would attend or how we could not wait to relax at the closest happy hour. When in the car we enjoyed the pounding base of secular music glorifying fornication, drugs, alcohol, even homosexuality. At home we feed our spirit more of the same only in music videos. Our lifestyle, our way of life, our daily routine was that of what we wanted.

Similarly, now yoked to righteousness the will of Christ should be infused in our every thought and action. Focusing on only "the big sins" or public acts like fornication, adultery, or alcohol abuse is not sufficient. We must strive for excellence in every thought and action.

When at work we should not only think of the task at hand but being punctual, honest, effective, and other aspects of walking in integrity. Taking a two hour lunch yet acknowledging only one hour on a time sheet compromises our burden to fulfill His commandments, yokes us once again to sin, and opens the doorway to additional demonic influences. When at home, the gossiping and use of profanity in private telephone conversations are subject to the same standards of holiness and should exemplify the One we represent.

Since birth we have spent our time fulfilling our own desires. As babes we screamed and cried when we desired the security and comfort of our mothers embrace. As children we fulfilled our desire to play at will leading to our teenage desire of adult things and freedoms. Until the time of salvation we naturally lived to gratify our flesh. This reality forces a conscious choice to implement the will of God in one's life. The more we practice fulfilling His will and yielding to His commandments, the more it becomes who we are, taking root in our very souls.

The more we cut away flesh and replace it with Christ the more our lifestyle glorifies God and not self. There is no shared space between light and dark, righteousness and unrighteousness, Satan or Christ. This, once again, speaks to the needed completion of the spiritual cycle we have discussed. After chastening the yoke of sin we have worn our entire life must be broken and the yoke of righteousness carried in its place. Deliverance has to take place.

When Am I Delivered?

I would love to say there was a single defining moment where the awesome power of the Almighty God manifested and overtook me, shattering every shackle and breaking every yoke that I dawned from my life of sinful rebellion. I would love to say that but it would not be entirely true. Yes, the work of our deliverance is a defined moment...or should I say was a defining moment. That moment was the work completed at Calvary and the awesome power of the

Almighty God did manifest as the sky turned black upon the death of our savior and His subsequent ascension to heaven. However, the reality is that as much as it was a process to ensnare and entangle you in sin, it is likewise a process to experience the full manifestation of the deliverance and destruction of the yoke of sin we carry.

There are some things to consider and understand when seeking to break off or unyoke yourself from the actions, habits, people, and spirits that have you yoked to the enemy, self, or the world. As you experience some of the points they will become your own defining moments full of revelation, wisdom, and testimony you can then use to bring others to the place where they through Christ remove their yokes.

Please understand the deliverance process is not often a pleasant one. Living a life in right standing with the Father is full of difficult choices. At times you may question why you are putting yourself through it. Suddenly the people you used to party with look like they are having more fun than ever before. The things you are sensitive to will be used as devices to discourage you, distract you, and dismantle anything positive you and God have built. With a yoke of sin you were in the hands of the enemy. You were his property in a way. He was conniving, deceitful, and manipulative, working hard to get the reins of that yoke.

Having no power to take them back, he will do all he can to get you to voluntarily turn them over to him. I offer you some strategies, cautions, and explanations from my personal and ministerial experience. I do not count myself a "deliverance authority," but in many areas I made it through and you can too.

1.) Do not judge your deliverance or process by another's.

Some say you know you are delivered or freed from a particular yoke when you no longer desire a thing. "God took the taste out my mouth" is a popular church cliché. I believe you know you are delivered when YOU know you are delivered. In other words, you are delivered when your mind understands, your heart believes, and your lifestyle reflects that you do not have to participate in that particular act anymore. Even though your flesh may desire it you choose not to.

As discussed previously, a yoke often leaves an imprint on your soul and some grooves run deeper than others. While you may know one person who was able to simply lay down their cigarettes never to return again, you find it difficult to walk pass a discarded cigarette butt on the sidewalk without a craving consuming your entire being. Likewise, while one individual's process returns them to the place they were delivered from (presumably for ministry) does not mean you were called to or capable of going back into the environment or around the people you were delivered from. Your process is your process and is dictated by your relationship with Christ and His will for your life. Just as you look different from another, so will your process.

2.) *Be confident in your relationship with Him.*

When we are born to parents and are raised to know them as mother and father. We are able to confidently walk in our understanding of who they are to us as well as what they can and will do for us. Years as their son or daughter teach us how to approach them with a difficult question, when is the best time to ask for something, even when to tell them bad news. We know everything from the best time to get what we want to their look of stress warning us to hesitate.

This is the same manner in which we should approach our relationship with the Father. As His sons we are to have access to certain benefits and privileges. How to access those benefits, when and how to approach Him, even understanding what He has for us requires experience being in His presence and time learning of Him. We are to become familiar with His character so we can identify His path and will and walk confidently through the minefields of the world.

We do this through continual conversation with Him and unwavering trust in Him. We must stand confident in the belief that He has our well-being in mind and that He does care about us. He is our Father and we are His children who He loves. Let go of any shame or condemnation about our past disappointments. Your confidence in Him and in who you are to Him will help carry you through the challenging times.

3.)   You ARE different.

When you accept Jesus as your Lord and Savior you may experience a progressive or even immediate difference in the things and people you will tolerate. You may become super sensitive to the things to the negative aspects of the things you once embraced. For example, a profanity filled conversations with friends may now make you cringe as if each word is burning a hole into your ear. The obvious absence of your verbal contribution cause acquaintances to proclaim, "You've changed."

Here is where the enemy lay in wait to see if the opinion of others will weight heavier than you new found relationship with the Father. Typically the younger and more impressionable and individual, the more challenging it is to withstand the perceived neon sign overhead flashing, "DIFFERENT! DIFFERENT!"

Here is something to consider. You ARE different. You are not just different in the 'God made us all unique' way. As someone who has chosen to walk with Christ and remain yoked to His will for your life, you have a different path to travel. There are things He wants from you that those who do not know Him cannot help with. In fact, they can hinder you and damage your progress. He has set you apart so the seed planted in you can have an opportunity to be nourished, grow, and bear fruit.

Once yoked to Christ it is no longer business as usual. You have been washed in His blood and no longer look or smell like the world. You are different and that is a good thing. The sooner you accept that fact, gaining confidence and strength from it, the sooner the opinions of those outside His will lose power over your thoughts, actions, and self esteem.

4.)   *Don't go it alone.*

The wonderful thing about being a child of God is that you are part of a family. Immediately your brothers and sisters number in the millions. Yet, enduring some of the issues discussed in this book can make you feel alone and as if no one could possibly understand.

Don't suffer quietly, alone, and in pain. The walk of a dedicated child of God is not an easy one. There is much to learn and the continual challenge of finding balance between the spirit, soul, and flesh. There will be successes and failures. You do not need to endure either completely alone. Join a bible based church that will help you develop and grow your relationship and not your religion. Surround yourself with like-minded people. Entrust your training to a competent and even well trained spiritual leader who will offer wise counsel.

You may find these three – a church, similar people, a leader – may solidify in your life through trial and error. Much like Christ places people in your path too does the enemy. The ones meant to travel with you will remain. You will find some are only there for a season. Their departure may prove painful and disheartening. Learn what He wanted you to learn from the experience and remain focused on His will for your life.

Whether people stay or they go, He has prepared individuals to cross your path at various points of your walk with Him and throughout the journey there is a global, kingdom family you are a part of. You are never alone. Please do not choose to be.

As I continue to walk with Him I learn more and more. I grow taller and stronger. I spiritually and naturally see things I could never have imagined if not yoked to Him. Until He calls us home the task is not complete. There is work to perform in the world for His kingdom. Our assignment is not up. He has a purpose for our lives. Remaining connected to Him will ensure it's not our will, but His will is done.